Beyond the Loss Breaking the Stigma of Depression and Suicide

IbbiLane Press
copyright ©2015

All rights reserved. No part of this book may be reproduced or utilized in any form or by any means, electronic or mechanical, including photocopying, recording, or by any information storage and retrieval systems, without permission in writing from the publisher.

ISBN-13: 978-0692563809
ISBN-10: 0692563806

Cover design by Sue Johnson of SLJ Photography

To everyone who has ever lost someone to suicide or considered suicide their solution.

Contents

Forward	ix
A personal note from Kellie Fitzgerald	3
Paul's Suicide by Susan Harlow Schott	7
This is my story, by Kristine Marie	19
Three calls that changed everything, by Jody Doty	29
A life touched by suicide, Kellie's story	36
In the jungle, by Denise Wisdom	43
Suicide: Thoughts, Facts, Fears Mary Kay Elsner – Spryte B.S. Psychology	49
From Lisa Van Slyke	58
Thank you for being a friend By Almetria Turner	61
"He Cried For Help, But Nobody Would Listen. A Friend To Everyone, But Himself" By Kimberly Bayne	73
Ms. Lydia, by Marc C. as dictated to Kellie Fitzgerald	84
Fade to Black, by By Kathleen Ann Grün McCarthy	92
Final Thoughts	97

FORWARD

 As a psychologist and life strategist, I have a special interest in human behavior and well-being. So when Kellie Fitzgerald asked me to pen the Foreword for this book, I was humbled and honored.

Suicide is a major health concern. According to the National Institute of Mental Health, over 41,000 people die by suicide in the United States each year. Death alone is a traumatic event. Yet death at the hands of oneself compounds that trauma, especially when the individual is perceived as sinful, selfish, weak, manipulative, shameful, or a failure. Because of the social stigma attached to suicide, many people refuse to seek help. Instead, they attempt a solo navigation of self-destructive thoughts and overwhelming discomfort in their own private hell.

Surviving suicide is a long and painful journey. The trauma of suicide has strong emotional repercussions for its survivors and for families of its victims. Caring for and supporting someone who has lost a loved one to suicide can be extremely difficult. This is especially true because not everyone grieves in the same way, and many people struggle with understanding the depth of such distress, as well as identifying meaningful ways of providing comfort and support. Families often disintegrate in the aftermath of suicide. Therefore, maintaining a strong support network is important and can make a significant difference in terms of dealing with intense grief and healing.

The associated stigma and reluctance to report suicide prevent us from seeking help or offering support. This book is a testament from those who are courageous enough to share their stories. It is a must-read for anyone whose life has been touched by suicide. These stories provide deeper insights into this devastating struggle, serve as a guiding light, and can help to validate your experience and maintain your well-being as you cope or help others work through complex feelings and emotions. The gentle wisdom of this book allows us to discover within ourselves the capacity and courage to make the seemingly impossible possible by making sense of suicide and creating new life and new hope as we do our part to find meaning, reduce stigma, and make the world a more compassionate place.

MARY CANTY MERRILL, PhD
Denver, Colorado
8 October 2015

A collection of very brave people came together to tell their stories in this book. Their stories were intentionally left completely "intact" with very minimal editing. Some of the co-authors have chosen to change names, others have not. It is my hope and the hope of the co-authors of this book that the stigma associated with needing help with emotional and mental issues is permanently broken.

We long for compassion and understanding for those who grieve someone who has chosen to end their own life. We hope they are afforded as much space and time they need rather than have to answer questions for which there really are no answers.

Also we hope that as a society we try harder to have the conversations about mental illness so that fewer people make the decision to end their pain by ending their own lives. It is our hope we all learn to love, take care of and respect each other and accept that often people are in great pain on the inside while smiling on the outside.

Further, that we make it easier for those people battling inner pain to find help without feeling like they are "less" for doing so. May you, our reader, never, ever feel such inner pain.

If you are in the United States and you are thinking about suicide as an option to stop your own pain, please call the **National Suicide Prevention Lifeline** at

1 (800) 273-8255

A Personal Note From Kellie Fitzgerald:

Recently I learned there is actually a World Suicide Prevention Day. This revelation has given me reason to pause and reflect on how my own life has been touched by the suicide of those I cared for as well as those very dark times when I myself considered suicide as an option. I know, to many of those who have come to know me over the past several years this might sound impossible. After all, I am now an incredibly happy person who delights in making life better for those around me. I've actually made a career out of helping people to feel better. But, I assure you there was a time this was not the case at all.

There have been many very dark times in my life and I've started over from scratch over and over again. I've been very sick to the point of almost dying and I've been very broke to the point of making "tomato soup" out of those ketchup packages you can steal from fast food restaurants. I've briefly lived in my car. I've skipped meals so my daughter could eat and I've done some things I'm not terribly proud of to pay my bills and put a roof over our heads. Along the way I've dealt with depression, sometimes better than others. About four years ago things became incredibly dark. I'd been sick again, requiring surgery and other treatment again, and on top of that there was a severe issue within the family I came from regarding money. It had gotten to the point where I became sick and tired of being sick and tired and decided I just didn't want to go on anymore.

The bravest thing I've ever done was tell someone how I felt and what I was thinking. That someone turned out to be my husband. That moment turned out to be the beginning of my own personal turning point. Just the fact someone knew how horribly I felt and how much pain I was in, yet still loved me enough to see me through that horrendous darkness made me think that maybe I could go on. Maybe I could even feel better. So, I started writing, first for just for myself. Then I wondered if maybe someone else could be helped by reading my story so I kept writing. Within weeks I had the rough draft of my book and within months it was published.

Today I have the most fulfilling life. Much more fulfilling that I ever could have imagined. This year in particular World Suicide Prevention Day really hits home for me. Last year at this time I was anxiously awaiting the arrival of my grandson. This September marks my first full year as a grandmother. Today, I am so very, very grateful someone cared enough about me to make me begin to care about myself. I would have missed so very much had I not made the decision life was certainly worth living. I also know someone somewhere, in truth many "someones", are now in the pain and darkness I was once in and my heart goes out to them. I've been there. I'm here today to say please reach out to anyone you can reach out to. Talk about what's going on in your mind. Talk about your pain. Please, believe things will get better. If you know someone who is currently battling with depression, don't wait for them to reach out to you...reach out to them. You just may be their last chance. You might just be saving someone's future grandparent.

Take care of each other always! We shouldn't need a World Suicide Prevention Day, but apparently we do and if having this day brings suicide to the forefront of everyone's mind it's a very good thing.

Paul's Suicide

By Susan Harlow Schott

I was an infant when my parents divorced. I lived with my mother, her parents and my brothers and sister. Being the youngest of four was not easy especially with the huge age difference. I treasured the times I could sit and watch old movies with my Mom. At school everyone talked about their parents. I was ashamed I didn't have a father. It made me feel odd. My two older brothers had their father still in their lives and he sort-of included my sister and I for birthdays and holidays.

At school one year was a Father-Daughter dance, I was about 13 years old, and, Pete, a family friend came with me to play the part of my father. I was sad. For my Confirmation at church I invited my father's parents. They had always sent me birthday and Christmas cards over the years. My mother would never speak of my father, but I knew she kept files on him. I knew something terrible had happened in their relationship. One day I went snooping in her room and found what no one would talk about. I was determined to uncover the mysterious secrets and why no one would talk about him. I went to the local courthouse and pulled the trial transcripts; imagine that at such a young age.

I knew my parents had started a driving school business together at one point and I knew the city, so I started with the phone book and calling places. I found it. A lady answered the phone and asked who I was. I said "I'm Paul's daughter" and when I realized what I had said, I quickly hung up the phone. Those were the days before Caller ID. I walked home from school as usual a few days later and had fixed myself a snack and was watching the television. There was a knock on my front door. I was told never to open the door when I was alone in the house. I looked through the drapes and recognized my father. My heart raced, my stomach hurt, I said, "Who is it?" He simply said "Paul." I didn't know what to do. My mind was racing. I knew who he was. What do I do? What do I do? He asked if I would go for a ride with him. I called my Mom and I did. It was fine. He asked me all kinds of questions and I told him I had Epilepsy and was taking medication. He told me he didn't believe in illness and only weak people were sick. He gave me an Olympic coin from Mexico that day. I stopped taking my medication. I didn't want to be weak. Mistake!

Over the next few weeks he would drive me places and ask me all kinds of questions. We drove to Daly City where he had an apartment, but we didn't go in, he just showed me where it was. We went to Joe's of Daly City and had a "Joe's Special." He took me to Tilden Park and we sat on a bench. He asked me to draw what I saw and he would do the same. I drew the clearing of trees with all their branches and leaves. He drew a single leaf. He was very talented. I wondered if he thought I was. He never said. Our perspectives were very different. He took me to John Muir Wild Life Refuge and while walking along the beach he picked up some kelp and offered it to me to eat, explaining the nutritional value of it. I passed. For my 16th birthday his mother, my grandmother Myrtle, bought me a 32-foot mahogany hulled sailboat that had a 5-foot keel. Her daughter, Sylvia, and her family lived in Saudi Arabia and had wonderful family time yachting. She thought it would bring Paul and I together. It was moored in Berkeley and Paul made me learn nautical knots, terms and compass navigation. He even had me sail from Berkeley to Angel Island using only the compass; I was not allowed to look up. We made it, but it was rough.

Soon my grandma Myrtle became increasingly weak and ill from age and passed. I rode in a limousine for the first time at her funeral. I met my Aunt Sylvia, Paul's only sister for the first time and my three cousins. We returned to the family house, people picked through things and said I want this or that. I found it offensive. I didn't feel like I belonged.

Then there was a terrible storm and my boat sunk. Someone had stolen the engine and it had to be crane hauled out of the water. My mother, a secretary, couldn't afford to pay for it so we took the paperwork to DMV and "junked" it. I was heart-broken. It was something I had that was mine, even if Paul was attached to it.

Time passed with no word from Paul. No involvement. I graduated high school and then married and had children. I tried calling Paul again. I left my professional "head-shot" picture at his house. I left messages of where I was performing with the band I was in. One day he showed up at a show. I was surprised and introduced him around. By this time I was getting divorced and sharing custody with my husband. Paul came to my apartment in Concord and asked me to go camping with him in the Sierras with the boys. My kids were 1 and a-half year old twins and a 3 year old. I was very uncomfortable with the suggestion. I knew he loved camping and being rugged. I knew he had survival skills and I would not have anything to worry about. I also knew everything would be a test. When I began to question the idea, he promptly left without a good-bye.

Again I was hurt. All I ever wanted was my father to want me and want to spend time with me. Life went on and I was empty. Wishing it could be different.

My kids were in high school and performing in the choir program. I received a call from Paul, his sister Sylvia had passed away. He invited me to her memorial service. The three boys and I went. Paul introduced me to family members who didn't even know I had existed. The night felt like it was the start of a new beginning. It was December.

Again I didn't hear from Paul. I was sad and empty not hearing from him. I left a message, unreturned. I tried not to think about it. It was always this way it seemed. I wanted some kind of a relationship with him and it seemed like maybe this time. My oldest son asked me what was bothering me. I said, "I've only just wanted a father who would love me for just me." My son said, "It doesn't matter what he thinks. We love you." I know that should have been it for me. I wanted it to be it for me. It wasn't. I remember thinking how wonderful and lucky I felt to have such a wise and wonderful son at such a young age.

Weeks passed and I was working on my computer when the phone rang. The voice asked me if and how I knew Paul. I was confused. I stammered a bit and said, "yes," "who is this?" The voice identified itself as a police officer. He asked, "How did you know Paul?" I said with great apprehension, "I'm his daughter." The voice said, "Your name and phone number were on a sticky note on his computer. He was found today in Wild Cat Canyon in Tilden Park where he hung himself. I'm sorry to tell you we need someone to come down and collect his personal effects." All of a sudden I felt flushed, confused, angry, frightened and unsure. My stomach hurt and I felt light-headed. Dazed I said, "Oh, okay. We'll be right there." After I got all the information on where to go I hung up the phone, speechless.

The first thing that came to mind was I'll never have a chance again. I felt robbed. Empty. Sad. Mad. What do I do? What am I supposed to do? We drove to the morgue. They would not let me see him. A few weeks later the officer escorted me to where his body had been found hanging in the tree. I left a flower there. I have not been back.

For months I pored over the papers I found looking for clues. He had sent a letter to his neighbor across the street and to the police department. The return address he used was his exact location and time of his hanging. He planned to have the police find him immediately. Unfortunately a young girl running through the park found him first. It must have been moments after. Her call came in at the same time the letters were converging. I spoke to the neighbors desperately trying to find any clue. They told me he'd had a stroke but with determination had fully recovered. They told me, he had been told he had to move out of his family home by his brother-in-law who intended to sell it. They told me he had tried to set the house on fire, but had failed. They told me his deadline to leave the home was March 5th. That was the day he picked. The day he was supposed to be out, and he was.

The tree he had chosen was a particular spot where he had spent a lot of time as a child and in scouting. It overlooked a creek in a very shady area. It was beautiful, secluded, and quiet. When the officer had taken me there I had taken pictures. I thought if I had them to look over there might be a clue to understanding. He had picked a very sturdy tree and branch. He had taken the time to trim all the little leaves and burs and minor branches so as to make the process as smooth as possible. It appeared he had climbed the tree and stood on the wide branch. Did he question his decision? It seemed he just stepped off. The coroner said he probably never felt a thing. It was instant. A clean break.

Initially packing things up and going through papers my sister helped me find my father's first family. Ironically the day of discovery was April 1st. When I called to contact my siblings they thought it was a joke. Now at least two of the three have accepted me and embraced me. The other doesn't want to even give me a chance because of the connection to Paul. So I have another empty place of non-acceptance.

After years of going through the papers he left behind I never found the answer. He was a very smart man, concerned with the origins of life. He believed in self-sustaining, growing his own food and living simply. He had started one of the first community gardens in Richmond, CA years before. He had relationships with UC Berkeley Professors and trained Chinese coming to study there how to drive and speak English. I found a variety of Asian gifts with many "Thank You" notes. He was developing solar for a sailboat he was planning to sail around the world. I found so many nautical and astrological charts. He did not spend money. He did not shop to increase his possessions. He lived among the belongings of his parents and those memories. He lived to explore his universe, the stars, and the migration of man.

Time has passed and I can't stop thinking of why. I have blame in me, and anger still. I wonder what could have been so bad? I know he went out on his own terms. Meticulously planning each detail. Was he angry? Did he feel alone? I was reaching out to him. Didn't that matter at all? I was a child ready to get to know him and love him. How much of me is like him? He intentionally kept himself a stranger, why? Why? Why? I'll never know. I'll never figure it out.

"Your soul was woven from the stardust of every galaxy in the universe; the love in your heart was spun from that celestial light; your path in life should be nothing more than a lighted highway back to that sacred place. In the vastness of the universe, you may feel insignificant, but in God's eyes it's the littlest of things that He cares about most. Never underestimate how beautiful or grand your seemingly modest little soul is."

—Robert Clancy, Author of The Hitchhiker's Guide to the Soul

This is my story

By Kristine Marie

There. Will. Be. Light!
Me depressed?!
Ha there's no way! I am positive, strong spiritual beliefs, faith, I can shake this off. "I just need to think clearly, everything is scattered and irrational, but I'll be fine.

I. Don't. Need. "Help." ~ I got this.
Those are all famous last words of a fool ~ this fool.

I don't know why depression surprised me so, no one else seemed surprised, well only that it had held off for so long. A very sweet counselor at a local mental wellness center explained rather well as she tried to grasp all that had taken place in my life since 2009, well really since 2004.

I will spare you all the details and give the "shortened" version. First I began to notice a numbness (yet painful) feeling in my feet, along with a feeling like my brain wasn't fully connected at times in 2004 ~ it progressed and began to affect my speech and I would mix up my words and I knew it but I couldn't correct it, a very strange and frightening feeling. It got to the point I could not ignore or make excuses for it. That was in 2009, I closed my property maintenance business, which I had owned and operated for 14 years and I LOVED my work! But I just couldn't do it anymore; I knew I was becoming unable to do the kind of physical work it required. Then my doctor and I went to work on figuring out what the heck was happening~ 18 months of aggressive testing and watching my health deteriorate, we had our answer.

In 2010 I was diagnosed with MS *multiple sclerosis* or as I call it *my body's bully! I was told by some wonderful specialists that there was no cure for MS and that the damage done could not be reversed at this time but that I could hold the progression off a little bit with certain medications. That meant no more surfing, skating, dancing or worst of all ~ no playing and running with my grandson! I was told I would need my walker forever and that because the relapse I was in I could expect to still end up in a wheelchair, everyone seemed quite surprised that I wasn't already.

This information was unacceptable to me! I wasn't going to just let this thing come in and wreck my life, I was still young and strong and I had things I wanted to do!!! I'll talk more about what happened after that another time, this is still the shortened version remember!?! Lol

Now I had family around that supported and love me dearly, I know that and I am ever so grateful for them. However there is a terrible aloneness with something like that. I didn't want to spend my days trying to explain this thing that had taken over my life and turned it not only upside down but inside out as well!

Feelings of "what do I do now? What can I do? What use am I? And the biggie ~ why did this have to happen to me!?! I had no answers. And for the first time in my life I felt useless, and afraid. Those are two emotions I honestly had never felt before in my life, I blame my Mother! She raised me to believe I was a miracle, a wonder, capable of anything I set my mind to~ but I hadn't set my mind on this. But I was determined to not live in that cloud of grey!

So, I went to work on strengthening my legs again, I mean come on ~ I had been so active all my life surely I could do something! During this time some very personal and emotional things happened too, some devastating, others glorious ~ like my grandson being born! I celebrated the good and wonderful, and "handled" the ugly, or so I thought.

In 2012 I surprised my general doctor and neurologist by using my cane more and no aids at all when I am at home! I only need my walker when I will be walking or standing for long periods of time. That's another thing I will talk more about later.

It was also during 2012 that my Father, who had been battling with terminal cancer for about a year by then made a very strong decision about his life, He was well into his 80's and had always been strong and independent ~ truly lived his life his way!

Anyway after having considering his new situation with the cancer he came to some conclusions 1) it wasn't going to go away. 2) The treatments he was taking to "prolong" his life were robbing him of who he had always been. 3) He would not have anyone "find" him vulnerable, helpless, etc. so 4) he chose to end his life just as he had lived it, on his own terms. All of us kids and our Mother, they'd been divorced for over 45 years, we all understood his choice, we didn't necessarily agree with it, or like it ~ but we understood him.

That's not always the case. And it is hard, and it still leaves so many questions. It also leaves so many things unsaid. And it added to the pile of crap others were going through. And then life goes on.

Now I said that we understood it, and I really think we all did, do. However, my eldest brother was closest to Dad and he misses his best friend, it hurts us all when the PGA tournament is playing, because that was one of their "big" things and we know he wants to call Dad and talk about how so and so made a great, or dumb shot~ or just get together and hang out. They were the most alike, both mountain men and both prefer solitude over lazy people.

And even when we went to tell our Mom, we got it, we understood why she cried. It wasn't about lovesick, it was about someone she had loved and had children with making that kind of choice, besides they knew each other, there was history and it hurt to think he felt this was the best way. And even I still can't quite bring myself to remove his number from my phone, that same sweet counselor that I mentioned before (?) Yeah, well she said that is my way of holding onto him because I wasn't ready to let go yet.

We hadn't been close, partly his fault, partly mine but that didn't matter we loved each other and we knew that at least I hope he did, I think he did. But I still, and sometimes I think the rest of us wonder if he really knew. Did he not know we would have taken care of him? That we loved him that much?

See I think that is the worst thing about suicide, even if the "reasoning" is understandable~ it still leaves those left behind to wonder....

Well now, back to the rest of this story ~ I have always been an over achiever and love to multitask, ha ha, so in June 2013 I was diagnosed with breast cancer. I feel so blessed 1) that we caught it early (stage 2b ductal carcinoma) 2) that where I live we have the greatest cancer treatment center and team of doctors are just incredible, efficient and caring, truly caring. Now eight surgeries, and nearly eight months of chemotherapy, I am doing really well. I felt like whew! I got this handled, life is good! And it is, I truly believe that!

That's why I was so shocked when a few months back that ugly old dark cloud started coming back around. How dare it! Didn't it know I had beaten all this crap and I wasn't done yet either, I was and am still fighting to get back to where I can run and play with my grandchildren ~ that darkness didn't belong here!

I was getting healthy and stronger and we were getting out to socializing again and I had/have so many who love me and cheer me on, this thing didn't belong! It was silly to be sad when everything was going so right! I had to shake this off. I was fine. I was happy, there was much to celebrate. This had to go. And that's what I did, I shoved it down and told it to go away, and pushed it under the carpet.

Yeah that didn't work too well. I remember the day (not the date, just what had been going on) I was sitting at my computer writing a short little note to go with a facebook poster with my own quote on it for a fabulous, amazing, energizing group I belong to that were featuring my poster. I was listening to the two women who founded this incredible wellness site that is the group, they were talking about "having a joyous life despite adversity and I was cheering them on and agreeing with every word they were speaking.... It was about a half hour show they were doing, and it was about 15 minutes in that I stopped writing because I could not see for the down pouring of tears.

I cannot even begin to find the words to express just how I felt in that moment, or all the days after. I tried to hide it, and I did a pretty good job of it, mostly. Everyone who loved me knew something was "on my mind, bothering me" but no one knew what. How could I say that after all I (and they) had come through, that now I was feeling so incredibly, overwhelmingly sad? I would cry uncontrollably for hours, hidden away. Then wash my face and pretend everything was great.

Then finally, I couldn't pretend all was well anymore and thankfully I was talking with a friend who suggested I get some help, which I did. First going to a psychologist, I did learn some valuable things from her, but more medication just wasn't what I felt I needed. I needed to address all that had gone on, yeah even mourn for the life I had before MS and the cancer and everything, lost relationships, relationships that have been deeply damaged. Everything.

Now I went a different route by using Emotional Freedom Techniques, or EFT (often known as

Tapping or EFT Tapping) and I am not selling anything here, what works for one may not work for all. But for me, this is working, and it's working on getting rid of rather than covering up the ugly thing we call depression. I will tell you right now, it is most effective (as anything is) when you commit to it completely. And that's hard! I mean really, really hard! But you only get out of it what you put in, energy wise.

After a couple of months of working on this, I am slowly getting back to me again and I cannot tell you how great that feels! It's not gone, I still have a lot of work to do on me, but I can see the light at the end of this tunnel, I am feeling joy again, I feel hopeful for the future, and I am even playing with my grandson!

With loves best energy,

Kristine Marie

Please, if you are in need of mental health services, please contact a licensed professional in your community. If there is an IMMEDIATE CRISIS such as a child or adult currently being abused, suicidal or homicidal thoughts or actions, or any other mental health emergency, CALL 911, or contact 1-800-SUICIDE (1-800-784-2433) or 1-800-273-TALK (1-800-273-8255).

Please do not wait! You have every right in the universe to feel better!

Three Calls That Changed Everything
By Jody Doty

They say things happen in threes and that's about all my anguished brain could latch onto when I received the telephone call that changed everything. Painful memories flooded my senses taking me back in time.

The news was shocking. My beautiful, hardworking, well-loved sister-in-law, Lee, the one with a wonderful husband and two beautiful children, who adored all things Oprah, cared deeply about others and made a mean guacamole at our family reunions, was suddenly and inexplicably gone from our lives.

Only days before we were laughing together at a chapel in Las Vegas where our entire clan gathered for an Elvis-style wedding. When I asked Lee how she was, I remember her briefly telling me about a medical condition that kept her in pain and the challenges associated with finding a medication that didn't have side effects that made things worse. In her usual easy-going manner, Lee quickly changed the subject to something more pleasant. "Enough about me" was her comment. Those words still float in my mind along with my own thoughts.

If only I'd pursued our discussion to a deeper level. If I had just asked how she was coping. If

I could go back to that moment in time, would things be different now? But life doesn't work that way. The words came in painful hindsight after hearing she had taken her own life. This is how suicide impacts, pain followed by endless questioning and no logic to be found.

You just can't fathom or wrap your brain around how an amazing, vital, beautiful woman can be here one day and then just disappear permanently from your life. My daughter is the one who noticed that Lee made a point of saying a special goodbye to each member of our large family after the wedding. That should have been a warning sign, but it was so subtle it was lost on us.

Yet, her goodbye hug and her smile are the last memories I hold in my heart of this loving, caring soul gone way too soon.

The second call came from my Mom letting me know that my cousin Ray had taken his life after a attending a family dinner. Ray did not have an easy life. He seemed to create challenges for himself by choosing relationships that were painful and trying to ease his stress by self medicating. He moved frequently and had trouble keeping a steady job. When his relationship ended, he took the opportunity to try to live more cleanly.

He asked his family for financial and emotional support and they were glad to see him start over again. Ray had high hopes for a new business and a new life. His enthusiasm waned and after a time he fell back into old habits. He lost everything including himself. His depression and shame hit a crescendo when he had to face his family letting them know the money was gone and so were the business and his will to live. Concerned about Ray's mental health, family members removed guns from the house, but they didn't realize he always kept one in his vehicle. He left the family dinner and this Earth.

When I heard about my cousin Ray, I was reminded of our childhood years, camping trips with my cousins, roasting marshmallows by the fire, Ray's mischievous teasing, and his energy. The thought that he will never see another sunset saddens me. In addition to Ray, my aunt raised three children while battling a very serious medical condition. She's is a fighter, a survivor who values and appreciates each hard-earned breath she takes. The differences between mother and son are marked. How difficult it was for my Aunt to receive that devastating news. It took all of her reserves, courage and strength to leave her sick bed and fly out-of-state to be with and bury her son. No mother should have to endure this kind of despair.

Our life touches others; we are connected. Within the circle of suicide, there is always more than one victim.

In addition to unanswered questions and disbelief, family members go through Hell to cope with the loss, pain, change and emptiness trying to reconcile the "what ifs" and "if onlys."

The "healing" process is never ending and excruciating. The trauma associated with suicide was best described to me as follows:
I'm not sure you ever heal all the way. I remember the original horror, which I played over and over in my mind hundreds of times, in painful detail, like watching a horror movie again and again. You numb to it eventually and it's not as scary as it was at first.

My feelings now are mostly frustrations. When something triggers a memory, I feel a fluster in my heart and temples. I feel the loss and I am frustrated that it is so permanent and unfixable. And then some mental defense system that I have developed pulls me quickly back to today and reality.

Those left behind try to continue living life the best way possible, but there are always reminders, triggers that activate--places the family visited, old photographs, words, songs, sounds, smells, even food. We try to stop the process, to eliminate the pain, but it always shows up like an unwelcome passenger in the family car.

My third call that changed everything came a few weeks ago while I was on vacation. It was my best friend letting me know our mutual friend *Lisa had taken her own life. I was dumbfounded. Not again. I could not believe it. Lisa was a force, a "salt of the Earth" type. Headstrong, savvy and powerful, she worked for public agencies for many years until she found her true passion late in life as a massage therapist.

Lisa blossomed while serving others. She adored spending time with those who benefited by her practical, no nonsense manner, her strong inner spirit and her compassion. To her friends, Lisa appeared to be doing well in her golden years. We socialized, went to dinner, the movies, and saw each other at gatherings where she always smiled, chatted and filled the room with her essence. But Lisa had secrets. None of us knew about the looming financial debt or the visits by officials looking to collect.

Once again the loss both devastated and riddled my brain with questions without answers. Why would a businesswoman who was intelligent, worldly and wise not seek help earlier or reach out to her family and friends to handle her financial hardship before it overwhelmed her? But this was not Lisa's way.

I've come to realize we aren't always privy to what is happening beneath the surface of another's life or understand fully the depth of the emotional, behavioral or physical pain they endure. True to character, Lisa took the situation into her own hands and left on her terms.

All three, Lee, Ray, and Lisa, departed my world in a split second, each arriving at the same ultimate conclusion--that there was only one answer, one way to deal with their situation. Families and friends have been left brokenhearted with painful memories that float behind the smiles in photographs and the everyday task of dealing with loss while honoring the memory of those we love and miss.

The best we can do is to support each other, offer hope, education and resources, talk about suicide, express our emotions, increase awareness of how it affects us, look for the warning signs. Above all, the call we can make is to reach out, to be there, to engage, to be kind to each other, and simply to love.

*Name changed to protect identity.

A Life Touched by Suicide
Kellie's story

You might ask why anyone would write a book about suicide and depression. Initially even I questioned whether or not I should put this book together. Having battled with depression myself though, I felt as though I have a duty to sort of pull back the shades and start the dialogue we really should be having and should have been actively engaged in for decades or longer. As for suicide, like many others my life has been touched by suicide. Looking back, it seems as though suicide has been present throughout most of my life.

The first time I remember hearing about a suicide was when I was a relatively young child and one of my mother's cousins hung himself. I saw how devastating that event was on my family. While I was seemingly too young to fully understand what had happened I remember thinking at the time that he must have been in extreme pain to have made his life-ending decision.

Years later when a classmate's father committed suicide I wrote what I hoped would be comforting words for this fellow student I barely knew. This lead to our teacher giving us extra breaks throughout my grieving classmate's first few weeks back in school so we could go outside where I would listen to him cry about how he wished his father had loved him enough to stay alive and how he couldn't cry at home because it would only upset his mother. I tried to explain how this wasn't his fault and told him it was ok and even good to cry so he didn't end up just burying this awful event deep inside. Still today I wonder at the teacher who allowed this student-to-student "counseling" to happen rather than become involved herself. Then again, maybe she was involved in ways I never saw. I just remember how odd it felt at the time for me to be allowed what I considered to be "special privileges" to go outside with my new friend while the rest of the class stayed behind.

Before I was a teenager my cousin's grandmother ended her own life by shooting herself in the head. (Only later would I learn this is not a very common way for women to commit suicide.) By this time I remember thinking surely there must be a better way to handle emotional pain than suicide. At the same time, the idea of suicide began to become oddly acceptable to me if there truly were no other options. I would spend hours thinking about why certain people seem to choose suicide and wondering if they had really tried to find other options to handle what I realized must have been severe emotional trauma and suffering.

So, by the time I was an adult I was fairly well acquainted with the notion of suicide. By the time I was 24 I had seriously considered it myself; the result of having been in a severely abusive marriage. When I found myself in the position of needing to choose a new employee for the company I worked for I had already been fighting my own demons for some time. As I've written previously in my book "When on the Road to Enlightenment, Don't Forget to Take out the Trash," the person I chose to hire was an ex-con who had obvious demons of his own."

Still, I decided to give him a chance.

I found Joe (not his real name) to be a very kind and quiet individual, and a very good worker who quickly and easily picked up new tasks. Unfortunately however the other people in the office didn't really give him a chance once they discovered his troubled past and time in prison. He was so terribly afraid of saying the wrong thing and so desperate for people to like him that he ended up alienating himself and really made everything so much more difficult that it could and should have been.

During this time I tried to help him ease into "life on the outside" and referred him to a company-provided counselor. Quickly it became clear he only wanted to confide in me so the counselor and I together began working with Joe, until he became comfortable enough to work with her alone. Unfortunately, Joe didn't show up for work one day. The following day the counselor went by his home and Joe said he decided to quit the job. Although we both tried to talk him out of his decision, by refusing to return to work the employer ended up terminating his employment.

Even though he was no longer working at this company both the counselor and I stayed in contact with him just to make sure he was OK. A couple months after he deserted his job I left for vacation. This was in the days before cell phones and I returned home to 17 phone messages from Joe, each one sounding more desperate than the last. My 18th message was from my friend the counselor who simply said "he committed suicide, call me." He had left a note saying basically that he was afraid of people and had grown tired of being afraid and felt the world would be better off if he wasn't in it.

For months I worked through guilt over not having been there for this troubled person I had come to care deeply about. At times I wondered if I had done him a great disservice by hiring him in the first place. Other times I wished I'd never left on vacation. Gradually I came to realize I had made what I felt was the best decision to hire him and had done my best for him by getting him into counseling.

I also learned if someone deeply believes the world is better off without them and makes the decision to end their own life, there truly is nothing anyone else can do to stop them.
There are many misconceptions about those who commit suicide. What I have come to know is those who choose to end their own lives are in great pain, they are not trying to "punish"

anyone-they truly believe those left behind are better off without them.

They are not being selfish. In their mind they are simply ending their pain. They've felt they've done their best in life and have come to believe it just was not good enough, so they see no option other than ending their own life. They believe they've become a burden and don't want to be a burden.

What I have found is once someone has made the decision and planned to end their life it is usually too late to stop them. If they really have made that decision they will make sure they are alone and no one knows where to find them until it is too late. Having been very close to making this choice myself I can tell you "yes" there is something that can be done to keep a depressed person from seeing suicide as a choice in the first place. This is the key I think. Keep depressed people from making the choice to end their own lives in the first place. I was very lucky that someone kept me from making that choice myself.

Many people fear the stigma of mental illness, so they never reach out for help. We need to change this. Depression is a very real and dangerous disease and lingering depression is almost always the underlying cause for any suicide or suicide attempt. It is time we have an open and honest conversation about depression and ALL mental illnesses.

It is time we remove the stigma associated with mental illness so those who need help feel no shame in asking for it. So those families living with someone with a mental illness so they can get the support they need. And, perhaps most of all, so no one will feel the horrible pain of losing a loved one to suicide.

IN THE JUNGLE BY DENISE WISDOM

Weeeeehhhhheee dee weeehhheeee a-weem-a-wum away, a weeemm a way, a weeem a way...in the jungle, the mighty jungle, the lion sleeps tonight. In the jungle, the mighty jungle, the lion sleeps tonight.

It was our song. The song that issued in the sweet beginnings of a summer full of fun and excitement. The night before she arrived, my sister and I would stay awake laughing with anticipation. Janet, our older cousin/"big sister" would be here soon.

It's now been over thirty-something years ago, yet the memories of those "Summers of Janet" are etched in my mind and soul. I can barely recollect where she slept during her few weeks of annual summer existence in our world. I remember her spirit of dance, music, art, love, and laughter. She directed, produced, and starred in our lives. One song, famously titled "In the Jungle", there we stood on our stage (the front porch); Lights, Camera, Action! Let the play begin!! Our childhood friends were our audience. After the performances, we would all gather on the front porch, now our "sitting ground". We would "create" our next play, imaginations abound while eating ice cream, potato chips, finger sandwiches and drinking "pop".

She was an expert in nail art, so I thought, creatively painting our little fingernails and toenails. We "played" store, school, jump-rope...all the summer outdoor games. She was a poet, a hair stylist, a fashion extraordinaire....so beautiful and cherished by all. Her dream was to become a model and to write poetry...she experienced both for a moment.

Flash Forward...Flash Back

My mother, in the back room, crying...wailing aguishly. My sister and I sitting on the pew, alongside my father. My aunt, Janet's mother, fainting at the casket. In an instant, she is scooped up in the arms of her son. Her tears streaming down her face. I remember. My father telling me to stop crying before I made myself sick. My efforts, to halt the ache in my soul, were useless. My big sister/cousin, lying in the casket. Yes, she looked peaceful despite the mark, of the wire cord, around her neck. In spite of the makeup, the "shadow" of the cord was apparent upon her skin. Peace had entered her soul, yet our souls experienced no peace without her. I cried and cried. No more "jungle plays", singing, candy, laughter...no more "Summers of Janet".

I never blamed her for leaving us. Every so often, sadness creeps my way when I reflect upon our times together. I understand she believed the pain was too deep and would not end. Janet's then two-year old daughter is now a gorgeous thirty-something. She became the joy of our lives and I became her "big" sister/cousin. Yet, she has emotionally and psychologically struggled without her mother. All of us "pushed through" the years without Janet. The memories flash in front of us; the pictures remind us of her charm, beauty, and kindness. No one discusses her suicide; the unknown of what could have been.

Flash Forward

A beautiful grand butterfly, magnificent in the color of sunshine, circles around me. I love butterflies!! In my ear, I hear a whisper, *"Butterfly Janet"*. I raise my hands; it flies away. As it leaves me, I softly hear the words,

"Weeeeehhhhheee dee weeehhheeee a-weem-a-wum away, a weeemm a way, a weeem a way...in the jungle, the mighty jungle, the lion sleeps tonight. In the jungle, the mighty jungle, the lion sleeps tonight".

"Letting go of grief is not about letting your loved one go. It's about making room in your heart to hold more love for them. If you have great grief, then you must have a very big heart too. Fill it with that love and share it with everyone."

—Robert Clancy, Author of The Hitchhiker's Guide to the Soul

Suicide: Thoughts, Facts, Fears
Mary Kay Elsner – Spryte B.S. Psychology

The year is 2009
5:21a.m. Phone rings: me "Hello"
Jennifer "Spryte, are you awake?"
Me "I am now, what's up?"
Jennifer "Nancy committed suicide"
Me "oh boy. She wanted to die....wow."

August 11, 2014 Robin Williams commits suicide in his home in California. After hearing the news of Robin's death I cried for the better part of an hour, called in sick to work and watched every movie of his I own... which happens to be all of them. I immersed myself in What Dreams May Come, laughed and cried at Aladdin and wept during Patch Adams. I grew up with Robin. I loved him like a member of my family and watched him from Mork to Mrs. Doubtfire.

Suicide is the act of intentionally causing one's own death (Webster- Merriam, 1988). I have mixed emotions about the act of suicide. As a scholar I see the need to understand why a person would feel compelled to take their own life and the ways to remedy it from happening. What pro active measures can we as humans do to help someone have a better quality of life to want to remain present in their body to finish this journey before experiencing the After Life? On the other hand, I support assisted suicide in cases of terminal illness where a person wants to end their life with the assistance of a Doctor to end their suffering, provided they are in a sound state of mind. Can we have it both ways? Should we?

In a perfect world people would live life to the fullest, set goals, live with the heart of a servant, and help others to achieve their dreams and goals. We would have a society built on love and helping one another and no one would want to take their own life prematurely. Reality is, life is not that way and each year people kill themselves in order to escape the pain of mortal life. The statistics are staggering, disheartening, and quite devastating to learn.

According to the American Foundation for Suicide Prevention (2015)
- An American dies every 12.95 minutes from suicide
- 90% of those who die by suicide had a diagnosable psychiatric disorder at the time of their death.
- Suicide is the 10th leading cause of death in the United States
- 2nd leading cause of death for ages 10-24
- 5th leading cause of death for ages 45-59
- Veterans comprise 22.2% of suicides

Reading through this list we see there are a lot of people taking their own life. I could be downer and say with the world over populated and food and water resources not being able to keep up with the ever growing population, maybe this is a plus for society. Shall I quote only the strong survive? Should we turn the other cheek and let people die if they want to? Or do we have a responsibility to our fellow human beings to help bring them back to the light when they are consumed by the darkness? What right do we have to try and talk someone down off that ledge if they have decided they want to jump?

Nancy was a very good friend of mine, whom I loved dearly. She had two children, a husband that adored her and friends who loved her energy and light. She seemed happy all the time and made jokes of things that were funny in everyday situations. She left a simple note which stated "I don't want to be in pain any more, may God forgive me. I love you all."

That was it. She stated she did not want to be in pain any more. She did not have a terminal illness and from the outside, physically she did not seem to be in pain. Inside however her Spirit ached. We had many conversations about her living for her children and her husband and she always said, "I'm just so tired of this life, I want to go home to be with the Father."

I was so angry with her for so long for leaving us, because I truly believed people who committed suicide really committed a horrible act by taking their own life and there was no way God would forgive them and allow them into Heaven or allow them to reincarnate and come back again to enjoy this gift of life another time. To love and live again, maybe be a healer or have another love of a lifetime with a soul mate or to find a friend, in a reincarnated life. My heart was bitter and closed to any reconciliation for a suicides soul. How wrong I was.

In 2009 my life changed for the better by going into the rooms of Narcotics Anonymous and admitting I had a drug problem. I got clean, had a spiritual awakening and recovered from my addiction. Now six plus years later I have obtained a Bachelors of Science in Psychology with an emphasis in Addiction and Counseling and I am currently living in Pennsylvania working towards a PhD in Psychology at PENN State University. WOW. Every day I walk around the campus which is one of the greatest academic institutions in America and I know I am blessed.

In 2010 I started seeking quiet time with the Creator in convents, hermitages, and spiritual centers. I am an eclectic with a relationship with YAHSHUAH MESSIAH (Jesus Christ) and I study the teachings of Buddha, Paganism, and Native American Teachers. During my retreats I would take a vow of silence for 3, 7, or 14 days and reflect and pray and study the Bible, Kabala, and other sacred teachings.

During these retreats I would fast from food and sometimes water for periods of time 24 hours, 72 hours, once for five days. During one of my fasts I was in the woods sitting near a river and thinking about death and suicide and the Creators view on it. It was revealed to me of the many Angels who serve to heal and assist us humans on our earthly journey. And the most amazing feeling came over me for those who had taken their own life.

After the death of the human body the soul leaves the body and is ministered by a special team of counselor angels who help the soul work through the issues and depression which led them to take their own life before it was their time to die. This place is not in heaven or hell it just is. I cannot find the words to explain how it was revealed but I will do my best to portray what was given to me in the quiet.

The Universe has a natural order to how Creator desires the stories of our lives to play out. We are given this gift of life to love and serve and be of assistance to those around us. Because the Creator is all loving, we as humans have been given free will and a soul to connect to this Spirit of the Universe. The human being is made of three parts body (the flesh, how we move), spirit (our mind and emotions, how we feel), and the soul (our connection to Creator and each other). When we have all three we are human. When we die the body dies but our Spirit goes on.

In Robin Williams' movie *What Dreams May Come* there is a conversation between Chris Nielsen , played by Robin and Cuba Gooding's

character about who we are when we die. Robin has died and Cuba is there to help him transition in heaven. Robin tries to walk on water and goes under and asks, "Am I really here"
Cuba: "What do you mean by YOU anyway? Are you your arm or your leg?
Robin: "Hardly"
Cuba: "If you lost all your limbs, wouldn't you still be you?
Robin: "I'd still be me"
Cuba: "So what is the me?"
Robin: "My brain I suppose"
Cuba: "Your brain is a body part like your finger nail or your heart. Why is that the part that's you?"
Robin: "Cause that's the part of me that thinks, that feels that is aware that I exist at all"
Suddenly Robin is elevated above the water to walk next to Cuba because he realizes he exists.
Cuba: "So if you're aware you exist, then you do." "Your brain is meat, it rots and disappears, did you really think that was all there is to you? Like you're in your house right now, you're in your house but that doesn't mean you ARE your house. House falls down; you get out and walk away." (Ward, 1998).

This is a beautiful illustration of the soul leaving the body once the human flesh dies.

So as I was sitting by the river thinking about suicide and how the Creator deals with humans taking their own lives it was so obvious that there are Angels who are there to receive those souls who leave this world early by taking their own life. After that I was not mad at Nancy any more. As I recall the feeling today as I write this chapter I still believe it to be true. Being a woman of faith I feel I am in tune with the Spirit which dwells inside all of us and I feel Creator is forgiving, even to those who take the ultimate gift that Creator gives us, which is life.

In my years of darkness as a drug addict there were many times I would do an obscene amount of drugs hoping to not awaken. Thankfully, Creator had a better plan for my life and today I am living the life I was meant to live as a Grad Student at PENN State University in the beautiful mountains of Pennsylvania. Moving forward when I hear of someone taking their life I say a quick blessing for their Spirit to find its way and continue on its journey. As a person I grieve and feel sad but I am no longer angry because I believe there is an all powerful and loving Creator who loves us and is looking out for each of us. And to the Angels who serve, many thanks for all you do.

Mary Kay Elsner –Spryte is an Author, positive hip hop artist and recovered addict. She can be found around the web and on social media sites. www.spryte.org

References

American Foundation of suicide prevention. (n.d.). Retrieved from https://www.google.com/#q=suicide+statistics+2015

Merriam-Webster. (1988, February). Suicide | Definition of suicide by Merriam-Webster. Retrieved from http://www.merriam-webster.com/dictionary

Ward, V. (Director). (1998). *What dreams may come* [Motion picture].

By Lisa Van Slyke

He always had expensive tastes. The thought flittered in her mind as her hand caressed the fine satin. So smooth and soft; only the best money could buy. The sounds of traffic outside distracted her for a moment. "Lunchers" she called them. Those who cram a whole day into sixty measly minutes; the working class on their lunch break.

If only I was joining them, she thought, never taking her eyes away from the creamy satin under her fingertips. Her eyes glistened as she slowly moved her hand across the flawless woodwork. The shiny surface of cherry-stained wood mirrored her exhausted reflection. Dark hair, deep green eyes, and a sadness reflected back at her. A pretty face, though.

"Just a few lines," she smiled. He always loved her smile. He was so good at loving her. And she never minded loving him back.

"Keep your mind on the task at hand," she whispered to herself. It was so easy for her to become distracted these days. Random thoughts would bombard her, relentlessly and furiously, reminding her of memories and scenes she would much rather forget.

She turned her attention back to the beautiful piece. He never was a big fan of brass, so the fixtures that adorned it was silver. Ornate carvings in the precious metal reminded her of a time gone by when she enjoyed taking paint to paper while she recreated images from her mind's eye. They matched the cherry finish beautifully. She glanced at her hand, noting her wedding ring. It was made of white gold. He surprised her on their wedding day with the ring set. Instantly, it brought tears to her eyes. She knew he couldn't afford it, yet he wanted her to have the best. "Only the best for my love" he would tell her when presenting her with a gift.

"I need to show him that these things are appreciated and cherished," she whispered to no one in particular.

She heard footsteps behind her. She turned to see a gentleman in a crisp, blue suit. His smile was friendly and inviting.

"This one will do just fine," she told him, turning back to the piece.

"Fine choice," noted the gentleman, moving toward her.

She watched as he slowly closed the casket. He turned and motioned toward the door. A bit relieved, she turned to walk away as a single tear fell down her face.

Shared by Almetria Turner
Thank You for Being a Friend

Thank you for being a friend was the popular theme song of the late 80's TV show, "The Golden Girls," but it was also the last thing that my friend called to tell me before he killed himself.

It was the summer of 1994 in which I first met "KJ" along with one of his guy friends. I was a sophomore going into my junior year in college and having the time of my life. I had met KJ's friend previously on campus during the spring semester, but I had never met KJ until now. One of my girlfriends was dating his friend at the time and had asked me to tag along with her while she visited him. The guys had just pledged one of the more popular fraternities on campus and boy were they proud members always sporting their colors. I could tell upon our first encounter that he was a true character and life of the party.

I don't think we were at his friend's apartment no more than thirty minutes before we both got the drift from my girlfriend and his friend they wanted to be alone. All I could do was shake my head and we both stepped outside so they could have their privacy. Here I was standing outside talking with KJ, a complete stranger in my eyes, but I felt as if I had known him all of my life. We were talking about any and everything up underneath the sun, including a picture of his new baby girl and before you know it, three hours had passed. Have you ever met someone where you immediately clicked and had a feeling in your heart of hearts you would be lifelong friends? KJ was that best guy friend for me. For some reason, I knew right then and there, I would love him for life.

The summer had passed and for some reason I didn't keep in touch with KJ. I don't know why we didn't exchange numbers then, but we just didn't. When we returned to campus that fall, I ran into him in the University Center where he was handing out flyers detailing the activities his fraternity was hosting for their Greek week. I immediately walked up to him and said, "Hey, I remember you. I met you at my friend's boyfriend's apartment this summer." He flashed his million dollar smile and said he remembered me. We exchanged more pleasantries, our phone numbers and from then on we were inseparable.

We talked every single day from that day forward mostly about stupid stuff like most 20 year olds do, except he was 2 years older than me. He had gone off into the navy, gotten married, and had 2 kids before he decided to go to college on the GI Bill. Once he completed his service, he became a part of the navy reserves for the benefits and extra money.

I would always see him hanging out on campus with his fraternity brothers and cracking jokes whenever he wasn't working. Sometimes, I wondered if he even attended class at all. KJ was a typical student in a non-traditional student kind of way. He had a family to support but his age and fraternal affiliation said otherwise. He was responsible in a lot of ways, but also irresponsible too when it came to being a student because he was always drinking, shooting off at the mouth saying something smart-alecky, and never going to class. I was more like his mother than his friend because my nurturing spirit felt like I had to watch over him and make sure he was ok. I was his protector, his tutor, and his voice of reason even though he wouldn't listen to me half of the time. We had a strange love/hate type of friendship, more so love, but it worked for us.

KJ had two different sides to him. The side he sensed everyone wanted to see and be around; the loud, boisterous, life of the party always drunk KJ, and the side that only a few of us who were lucky enough to get to know; the sweet, loving, down to earth and intelligent KJ. It's hard putting on two masks for the world to see when you think they would only like one...the wild one. No one should have to wear a mask in order to do this thing we call life, but people use them to hide the very thing that might expose and eventually defeat them in the end.

I could tell he was fighting some inner demons and low self esteem issues hence the wilding out and seeking validation from people. He was short in stature but tall in personality, very handsome, narcissistic, and a flashy dresser. It wasn't like he wasn't loved by his family and friends, but what I found was missing was the love of his true self. The outside world would say otherwise, but the dark places knew him well.

I eventually graduated and went on to grad school. He ended up getting a divorce, moved away, remarried, had kids, and became a successful business man. Even though he had moved away, we kept in touch off and on through the years or whenever he would come back to visit his family. There was a period of time where we didn't talk at all due to a misunderstanding, but my love for him ever left me. After all, we had been friends for close to 17 years by now. Life seemed to be going great for KJ until tragedy after tragedy began to hit close to home.

Family deaths and unfortunate life events surrounded, barricaded, and smothered his battered soul. He moved his family back home to try and start over by picking up the scattered pieces of his life, but he was never the same. It was the summer of 2010, when we reconnected at one of his fraternity events after not talking for years (he always had a stubborn spirit) for we had picked up from where we left off as if we never skipped a beat. Seeing him truly brought a smile to my face because I had really missed my best guy friend. We were like two peas in a pod again.

It was in God's divine plan that we were able to meet and work on our friendship for what was to come in the upcoming months would be devastating to say the least. What was hidden behind his million dollar smile and awesome words of advice, except for when it came to himself, was a soul that worked day and night to avoid the feelings of the hurt and despair that was crying from deep within through his times of loss. He had quit drinking years ago only to pick it back up again. I had no doubt his love for his family and friends, but when one walks though the valley of the shadow of death, it's hard to pull them out of it.

I had reached out to him on several occasions in trying to get him help, to read self help books or to go to church with me but to no avail. I could see that he was getting thinner and thinner from not eating. He was already a small man, so he couldn't afford to lose any more weight. I would invite him over to eat and would send him away with plates of food. I had been there with him through every celebration and every tragic moment for the past 17 years. We had our share of laughs and our share of cries. I have never seen him in such disarray nor with this much pain in his eyes. I just knew that this period in his life would be another hurdle he would manage to jump victoriously over just like had done with all of the other hurdles in his life. Little did I know there wasn't any truth to what I had believed would happen. He had spoke about death and the pain that he was going through, but not to the point where I thought he would harm himself. I knew he was depressed but I didn't know how far down the rabbit hole he had gone. I wasn't a licensed psychologist. I didn't recognize that these were signs of suicide and deep depression. I just knew I was his dear friend of 17 years who wanted to take his pain away.

During the holidays, he isolated himself from his friends and family. I remember begging him to at least spend the holidays with me or at least with some of his loved ones. I was so happy to find out he did reach out to one of his closest fraternity brothers and had spent some time with him and his family.

As I stated before, we had a strange love/hate relationship. Another misunderstanding had taken place where I said enough is enough. I walked away from our friendship. He was never apologetic in nature and I had finally gotten enough guts this time around to walk away because I was tired of him taking advantage of our friendship. I was the one always giving in whenever we would have a disagreement.

Two months had passed during this time where I heard nothing from him, but I always kept a tab on him because I was still concerned about this mental health and well being. I had gotten a cryptic text from him stating that he was sorry for all the things that he had said to me for someone had pointed out the error of his ways. He had never apologized to me before in the 17 years in which I had known him. He also said there wasn't any need to respond to the text. KJ was still being KJ in the end where he still had to have control of the situation even after an apology. So, I granted him his wish but I have regretted that decision ever since because less than two months later, I had gotten the last phone call I would ever receive from him.

I was in school part time working on my third degree and we were coming off of spring break. I remember sitting in my car waiting for my class to start when I saw his name and number pop up on my cell phone. A smile came across my face as I answered the phone. He called my name out and I said yes. Then he spoke the last words I would ever hear his voice say to me. He said, "Thank you for being a friend." I said you're welcome sweetheart. Then he hung up the phone in my face. That was the longest 15 seconds in my life.

Immediately, I had gotten an eerie feeling in my spirit. I sent him several texts asking him was he ok and I never got a response. I called my sister and I told her that I heard from KJ but he sounded suicidal and depressed. I hoped he wouldn't do anything stupid because of the children. She said all I could do was pray for him and that I've done all that I could do as a friend. So, I said a small prayer and went to class.

After I had gotten out of class three hours later, I called both of his cell phones but he didn't answer. I didn't have any of his family members or friend's phone numbers to call. Besides, how do you call them and say, "Hey, I think he is going to kill himself." After all, it was just a feeling I had but I quickly doubted myself because I didn't think he was capable of doing such a thing. He knew how it felt as a parent to lose a child. If he considered it, how could he do this to his parents, wife or children? I didn't think it was possible, but I had to realize everyone has a breaking point.

Later on that night, one of my girlfriends had called me because I was helping her plan a game night that was taking place at her house over the weekend. I answered the phone and she said hey. I didn't give her the opportunity to say anything else because the next thing that came out of my mouth was, "Please don't tell me he killed himself." She said, "Yes he did." I hung up the phone and started crying because for some reason I knew he was gone earlier that day. My friend was divorced from one of his fraternity brothers so that was how she had gotten the news of his passing. She knew how close we were and had called to tell me.

The next couple of days were very hard for me. I would repeat those same words over and over in my head, "Thank you for being a friend." At the end of his life, I felt as if I was a horrible friend. I let my pride get in the way instead of calling to check on him. I had blamed myself for his death because I felt like I didn't do all of what could have been done to save him. All kinds of crazy questions raced through my mind as to why I didn't try harder to reach out to his friends and family. Why didn't I just pick up the phone to call him instead of sending him a text asking if he was ok? Was there anything I could have said or done to make him change his mind?

I had fallen into a quick depression myself. I remembered wanting to get in the casket to comfort him and whisper to him everything would be ok. He wasn't in anymore pain. There were no more people to please or masks to wear. I had gained 20 pounds in 3 months because I used food to fill the pain of his loss. I didn't care what I ate or how I looked because my friend of 17 years was gone. You see, I was in the middle of a weight loss journey myself and it abruptly came to a halt because I figured what was the use of it now. I was missing my friend.

It wasn't until I had spoken to a friend of mine who was a school counselor, where I talked with her informally about grief counseling. After telling her his actions and the conversations we had a few months before his death, she said they were warning signs of someone who had suicidal thoughts. I didn't know. She said once someone who is at their breaking point, rarely in these types of cases; there is no turning back because they have already made it up in their minds as to what they were going to do. It wasn't my fault. I had to break free of the guilt, hurt and pain to the point where I had to realize he was gone, but I was still here. I had my own life to live and I was taking it back one day and one pound at a time.

Eventually, I had to forgive myself because I knew I had done all that I could do. I had been an awesome friend of his for 17 years. The counselor said by him calling me to say goodbye was his way of letting me know he loved and appreciated me for all that I had done as his friend. He was freeing me from feeling guilty for the decision he had made on his own. A sense of relief overcame me but it still didn't take away all of the pain.

A few weeks after he was buried, I decided to go visit him which was a first for me because I have never gone back to a cemetery site, even for my relatives; but for some reason I did it for him. I didn't want him to feel alone. I had a little talk with him and even told him how angry I was at him for putting his friends and family in this horrific situation of doing life without him. People say time heals all wounds and it does, but the scars are still there. Also, I'm blessed enough to have beautiful memories of my dear friend as well. As I was thinking of the different stories, adventures and conversations I had with him over the 17 years of our friendship, it dawned upon me during one of our conversations many years ago, he told me he didn't think he would live to see 40. The bible says, "There is life and death in the power of the tongue." He didn't. He died at the age of 39.

"He Cried For Help, But Nobody Would Listen. A Friend To Everyone, But Himself"
By Kimberly Bayne

At 12 yrs. old the last day of 6th grade, the thrill of summer break, sleep overs, hanging at the pool with friends and spending the weekends at the skating rink was the only thing on my mind as I rode the bus home that final day. My 7th grade year wasn't even on my mind, it was summer time and that was all that mattered.

When the phone rang as usual I bolted to pick it up just knowing it was my best friend calling to make plans. It wasn't her, it was a man on the other end and he started asking all kinds of questions about my family and if my mom still worked at the place they had listed for her. I was answering all the questions, when my sister came running out telling me not to answer any personal questions (by the way my sister is 10 years older than me). After I hung up the phone and had to listen to her growl at me for about 5 minutes on how never to answer personal questions to a stranger, when the phone rings again, this time she wouldn't let me answer it. I could tell by the look on her face that something was wrong, she told me that we needed to go to mom's work. When we arrived, I noticed how the others that worked there looked sad, one of the ladies that worked with my mom took my sister upstairs and made me sit by myself. What seemed like an eternity later mom and my sister emerged from upstairs, mom's face red and tears streaming down her face, I looked at my sister I immediately knew something had happened, something was very wrong.

My sister drove us home and mom hadn't said a word for a few minutes when she turned to me and pulled me on her lap in the front seat of the car. The words that she spoke to me are forever etched into my mind…. 'You know your daddy loved you, right?' She needn't say anything else,

I knew my dad had died.

When we got home I ran to my room and just cried and cried.

I can vaguely remember the days that had passed, I remember hearing my mom crying, I can recall some telephone conversations she had, I was so immersed in my own pain that I didn't care what anyone else was going through. I cannot though, recall the specific moment that I heard that my Dad had taken his own life, maybe it was due to shock, I am not sure.

What I do remember is the pain, the anger, the bitterness and the feeling of why…did dad not love me, why would he do this, were we not enough, was he not happy…the questions running through my mind were endless.

In the days to come my mom had to make arrangements and she had to leave me, you see my dad had committed suicide in Canada in his car, and mom, my brother and a friend had to go there to get all of his belongings and him. Mom had him cremated, and on the way back from Canada she dropped him off in Maine and had him buried. It was what he wanted…to be buried in Maine and mom didn't have the money to do it all, so there was no funeral, there was however a memorial service at our church.

Dad left behind a few letters, one left at the scene, one that he mailed home to us and one that he sent to his work.

His final words he wrote were…
"He Cried For Help, But Nobody Would Listen. A Friend To Everyone, But Himself"

This man, had suffered all his life thinking he wasn't enough, that he wasn't loved.

Rewind 50 years prior to his death. His mother had gotten pregnant with him when she was young, and back then the only thing to do morally was to get married. His father was an alcoholic and abusive. My grandmother blamed my dad from the moment of his birth that if it weren't for her getting pregnant with him she would never have had to marry his dad. They later had 5 more children. One of which died at a young age and my grandmother made the comment that it should have been my dad that died not his brother. My grandfather would take off and not come around for a while and then show back up when it was convenient all while leaving my grandmother to take care of the children. She took that out on my dad, I guess because he was the eldest and the one she resented.

My father left as soon as he could, joined the Navy and married had a child or two and then took off and found another woman and would get married and have more children. This happen a few times. We aren't even really sure how many of his marriages we legal. He couldn't hold a job for long, because he was constantly looking for something, never finding it. His real love was Radio, he was an announcer and station manager at several Radio stations.

Before you judge him, remember this was a man who was emotionally abused as a child. He was only looking for love and the feeling of being enough....to which he never found. Not realizing that he only needed to go within and know HE was enough, but when are told over and over as a child you are worthless, well that is the way you feel. Children learn what they live.

Fast forward...I struggled as a child, a tween, trying to find myself and come to terms and cope with the loss. The struggles of a tween into a teenager are difficult enough and then you add the loss of a parent especially to suicide can lead a child down a dangerous path of self-destruction, rebelliousness, worthlessness, anger, bitterness, resentment and more...oh and don't forget added to the mix, puberty. I can tell you this because this is what I lived, what I felt…all these emotions swirling around leaving me confused and utterly lifeless. Walking through my teenage years where honestly most of the time I just didn't give a SHIT! I was a rebel with a cause. In my mind I had an excuse to act out, I was lost, angry, bitter and hurt and that gave me every right to act the way I was acting. I didn't care if I got into trouble with the law. I certainly didn't care what my mom was going through; because she wasn't me, she had no idea how I felt. Getting mixed up with trouble making boyfriends, running away from home, oh the list is endless.

My mom did what she could, she loved me the best she could and she took me to therapist and counselors all to which did no good. I was on the fast track to self-destruction.

I myself was feeling worthless, feeling that my dad didn't love me enough to want to stick around. What did I do that caused him not to want to see me grow up? So I rebelled.

At 17 I got married, because that made me feel loved and who knows what else. Needless to say the marriage didn't last and 7 months later at 18 I was divorced. I couldn't hold a job (a lot like my dad) and was fairly promiscuous. I was all over the place, always looking for love and acceptance, again a lot like my dad.

At 19 I got pregnant and married a man whom I

didn't love, but we were going to build a life together and a family. I had my son at 20 and finally felt worthy, I looked at this little guy and finally found purpose. But, deep inside I was still angry, I was still searching. We had 2 more beautiful children and then divorced. I was still struggling inside. My children were everything to me and I wanted to make them feel loved and worthy every second of every day. Keep in mind I couldn't feel that for myself though.

I got re-married to a great guy and although the relationship was great still something was missing. I still had this anger and bitterness and was just an angry person who sometimes, I didn't even want to be around. About 10 years into our marriage some serious stuff happened, and it caused me to take a very long hard look at myself. Then one day, after all this confusion and anger, strife, cheating, failing business, death and not caring if I lived or died....I woke up! It was like I was hit with a bolt of lightning. And everything was different. My spiritual awakening was in full swing. I had been a very spiritual child and I felt had a very special relationship with God until my dad died, then it seemed as though everything got a little fuzzy after that.

During this time of confusion, I watched my grandmother pass and I had the most amazing and spiritual experience. As she took her final breath, something told me to look over my shoulder and as I did, I saw my grandfather with his hand stretched out for her, I watched her rise and walk and take his hand and then they turned and walked off. I was given a gift that day, not only the gift of watching that, but the gift of opening my heart again, the gift of seeing with my heart and not my eyes. After that day everything was different. I saw things differently, felt things differently and experienced things differently. I was awakening from what seemed like a long deep sleep.

I see! The anger and bitterness is gone, forgiveness and love in its place.

It took so long for me to come to terms with the suicide of my dad. Today, I see my dad as a hurt little boy who only wanted to be loved, who was so destroyed by his childhood that he couldn't find peace.

It took years be able to understand and forgive, not only my dad, but my grandparents as well. I had to see them as hurt souls, ones who were tormented at a younger age as well. They carried that into their parenting and it created so much pain, they lived what they learned, what they grew up with. This horrible cycle of pain that is passed down from parent to child.

Forgiveness and mercy is so very important in life. Being unforgiving keeps you imprisoned in anger and bitterness and you cannot be free.

My dad is very important to me, he taught me so

much without even meaning to (or maybe that was the way that it was meant to be, God always has a plan). He left me confused and angry, but taught me so very much and for that I am forever thankful.

We as a society need to understand and realize that words, especially to a child hurt, words can leave a lasting mark on a child mind and create a belief system that just isn't true. We need to build our children up into beautiful beings that will continue to love and not ones who will need therapy to recover from their childhood.

This is the most important thing that I want you to take away from this... treat your children with love and respect, build them up and teach them they are beautiful both inside and out, that they are worthy every day and in every way. Children should not have to recover from a childhood, they should not have to go to therapy to deal with how they were treated as a child. Children are precious and they should be treated as such. They will grow into the next generation of leaders...help them be good ones.

I write this to help break the stigma attached to suicide. Those who take their own life are not selfish, they are not cowards. They have a disease of the mind. There is something lacking, something missing inside, they are lost, scared and confused and they feel there is no other way out of it. There are usually signs, if someone plays close enough attention. The more awareness we create around this, the more likely we are to save lives.

As I began to write down the story of my dad's suicide, I was taken back to a time and place that was long forgotten. I was transported in time to that 12 year old girl whose feelings were all over the place. I experienced feelings that I thought were long dealt with, I was wrong. It took me to a very emotional place, one that was needed; a place of vulnerability and a childhood trauma that forever altered the course of my life.

As I was writing, tears streaming down my face...it hit me...it was supposed to be now, not 20 years ago and not 20 years into the future...but today. This moment, all the events of my life have brought me here. To this magical place of healing and of Love. I feel my Dads presence as I write, I feel his Love for me and I know he is and has been with me, watching over and helping to guide me.

I believe that everything happens for a reason. Was it meant for my dad to commit suicide? I can't say for sure, but what I do know is that it wasn't the first time that he had attempted it, he had tried several times before. If one of those times he had succeeded, I would not be here to share this story, because there would not be a story for me to tell.

I Love my Dad. I am Grateful that this man was my Daddy.

Letter from Dad:

"Words cannot express my shame for what I am about to do. I've hurt so many people in my life that it just can't go on any longer. You don't deserve to be hurt anymore. I've lived my life pretty much the way I've wanted to, selfishly, so it is time to get out of everyone's life, and stop the hurting. Sure, you've heard that before, but you won't hear it again.....

I hope Kim doesn't take it too hard....she doesn't have too many friends, I tried to be her friend, but I went about it wrong I guess.

I'm tired.

If there is a hereafter, we might see each other again, but I doubt it....

You are still young enough to get someone else, I don't care if they do get the house.

Why couldn't people listen to me as I cried for help."

My Lydia, by Marc C. as dictated to Kellie Fitzgerald

Lydia was my everything. We were very young, very much in love and very much looking forward to the future. She was smart, witty, and beautiful; everything anyone could ever want in a wife. I could always tell when she was really happy because she would sing. She had the most incredibly angelic voice; a voice that would wrap itself around you and make sure you knew you were loved. I still miss that voice.

When we found out she was pregnant we were overjoyed. While the timing was far from perfect it really felt like we were blessed. Gleefully we went shopping for baby things and began to set up a nursery in our soon-to-be-cramped tiny house.

At first everything was going along smoothly. One Sunday morning I made breakfast as Lydia took a shower. All of a sudden I heard a gut-wrenching scream and a thud coming from the bathroom. When I reached her, she'd passed out in a pool of blood. I called 911. By the time paramedics had her on the stretcher and in the ambulance she had been revived. I rode to the hospital with her even though they advised against it. I knew she needed me.

After what seemed like an eternity in the ER and oh so many tests, Lydia's doctor came out and said I could see her briefly but they were prepping her for an emergency hysterectomy and our baby, a girl, had been lost. It all seemed like a nightmare. They assured me she would recover and be fine - we could always adopt.

As I explained to family and friends what was going on, that somehow she'd suffered a rupture of sorts in her uterus, her sister offered to be a surrogate and others said we could always adopt. As horrible as this was it seemed certain we and most of all Lydia would get through it.

What should have been a three day stay in the hospital stretched to a week when Lydia refused to eat. Finally a Psychiatrist was called in and between the pharmaceutical cocktail he prescribed and my constant begging she began to eat. I had rented a storage space and moved all the baby-related items out of the house. After ten days they released her. I put together a schedule for family and friends so someone would always be with her at home. I took off work. After about a month I had to return to my job and everyone else needed to return to their lives. After all, Lydia seemed OK. Everyone said she would be just fine and seemed to be handling everything well.

I knew different. That angelic voice was silent. I talked to the Psychiatrist. He said as long as she kept taking her prescribed meds she would be fine. I wanted to believe that. I desperately longed to believe I would once again have my Lydia back.

As time went on she did seem to be getting better. I even got her to go out with me - dinner and a movie just like old times. Still she seemed a little distant. Certainly better but not the same.

As the next three months stretched by and I knew her original due date loomed large ahead of us I once again reached out to family and friends so she would not be alone. It's funny I didn't understand then why I wanted to make sure she was never alone I just knew it was very important someone stay with her constantly.

Finally the day came and I couldn't get out of work. No one could be there constantly. There was a four-hour gap of time when Lydia would be alone on that day. In my position at work no one could cover for me. I begged, I threatened to quit, eventually I did walk out. Lydia had been alone for just over two hours when I walked into our house. I found her on the floor in the room that was to be our baby's room. Beside her was an empty fifth of vodka and three empty bottles of her meds. I tried in vain to resuscitate her but my Lydia was gone. One of the paramedics who arrived had been one of the first responders the day of her miscarriage and tried to console me. He said he'd never seen two people so desperately in love as we seemed. Clutched in her hand was a note which said "I love my baby so much and I am so sorry I wasn't enough."

This angelic voice is forever silent.

This was fifteen years ago and some days it still feels like yesterday. I've moved on and remarried. I have two children now one of whom inexplicably reminds me of my Lydia. I will always love her. My wife knows this and accepts it. It was through her love I began to put my life back together again.

Retelling my story has reopened old wounds and tears stream down my face. I had to stop writing because I could no longer see the paper. Finally I convinced Kellie Fitzgerald to write it down as I dictated. I can tell you that yes, absolutely you can move forward with your life after a catastrophic loss. It is not pretty. It is painful unlike any pain you've ever had. You must be resolute in your efforts. If you are, you will get there. There is hope. Some days you need to struggle to find it but find it you must.

I hope my story helps someone else. I hope Lydia's life and death helps some other couple do better than we did. I hope all of this makes people really sit up and take notice of when someone they love is not right even when they are pretending to be. I knew she stopped singing. I don't blame myself anymore but still a part of me wants it to be known that if you love someone and they stop doing something they love...more needs to be done than simply prescribing a pharmaceutical cocktail.

Right now let's make the decision to pay closer

attention. To have discussions none of us wants to have. To make sure no more angelic voices are silenced.

To my girls: I love you and know I will see you both again one day.

"When you're mired in the shadows of despair, know there is always a higher light source behind any darkness; you just have to turn yourself around to see it."

—Robert Clancy, Author of The Hitchhiker's Guide to the Soul

Fade to Black
By Kathleen Ann Grün McCarthy

The phone rings. It's her husband. She expects it to be a normal conversation but instead, she is thrown into slow motion. Something has happened. Something devastating. People she loves are in gut wrenching pain. She is in gut wrenching pain. The wonderful, beautiful life she has worked so hard to create has just changed in heart breaking ways and it will never again be the same.

Fade to black.

Random noise and misty grey scenes.

Fade to black.

Her eyes flutter open to bright sunlight. She takes a deep breath, like it was the first one she has taken in a long time. She looks at the clock and sees that she has slept long into the morning. It's the first time that has happened in a while. The events of the last month flood back in – the one precious moment of forgetfulness has passed once again. Its respite is gone for today. Reality is once again, real.

It's almost June now: the last time she looked it was mid-April. Last time she looked, spring was just a couple of weeks old. Summer approaches now. It feels as though summer will arrive before she actually gets out of bed. She wonders when she began sleeping so long, it really isn't in character for her. Life is usually so full of things to create, to smell, to see, to experience – too full of fun to spend it sleeping. Yet sleep is demanding large amounts of her time now. She doesn't have the energy to do much else anyway.

It's not just her. So many people are hurting – dozens of people have been affected. Many have an even more difficult road to travel. She reminds herself hundreds of times a day to not be selfish here.

In the quiet corners of her mind, she begs the Universe to just let things go back to normal. Please let this all just be a bad dream...

She hopes. Hope is all she has. Hope is enough. It's enough to begin the process of recovery. Hope is enough to help her get out of bed and begin the day. It's enough to help her begin creating a new perfect life. Not all at once. Not tomorrow. Not quickly. But at some point in the not too distant future.

She plants things. She cleans things. She eats lots and lots of ice cream. Whatever it takes to find just a little bit of relief from the pain. Whatever it takes to maintain hope that life will someday be good again.

Fade to black...

It all sounds like a bad movie right? And yet

many people, every day, all over the world experience something like this.

This time, it was my husband and I. It all started with a phone call from Peter who was away on business in Budapest. His youngest son had taken his own life in what appears to be a fit of rage; but it is all of course, speculation…

Every single one of us will experience something like this bad movie at some point in our lives. The reason I am writing about this today is because I want you to know there is hope. And there is hope in places you wouldn't expect.

In the past, I had always avoided saying much to those in grief. I had this story running about how they didn't need my interruption and I didn't need to try and get some attention from the grieving folks. I had always thought it was a private matter that folks probably wouldn't want to share.

Boy, was I wrong. When my husband and I were on the receiving end, I found the mountains of condolences comforting and I don't mean in passing. There are still moments when I draw on all of that energy.

And I think that that is where hope began. I don't mean in the moment but a little later, the energy we received from everyone made a difference when we were ready to begin trying to get back to life. That energy was all piled up and waiting for us.

I will never neglect to send what I can to grieving friends ever again. Now I know – really know – why community is important in those sad circumstances.

InGratitude
Kat

Final Thoughts

By Annette Rochelle Aben

You did all you could, or all you knew to do. This statement applies whether you have thought about, or attempted suicide as much as it does if you have ever been around someone who has told you they were contemplating, had tried or shortly thereafter, DID attempt suicide. Perhaps they were successful and left this physical world at their own hand. Regardless of the scenario and regardless of what you did or did not do or even could not do, remember please, that you did all you could or knew to do at that time.

Please bear in mind that if something you were to have said or done, were to have turned the tide of a particular situation, then it would have happened. Often times, it is what we are least aware of, the smallest of gestures, simplest of words or even our silence that make the greatest impact. And of course, we may never know if it worked or didn't, even if for a brief and shining moment. However to beat yourself up over the way you think it "should have gone" is counter-productive as to why you wanted to help in the first place; to stop someone from harming themselves.

Give yourself a hug, right now. Even if the only way you can do this is with your mind, then say something nice to yourself. Perhaps the only nice thing you can think of to say, is to repeat the last nice thing you heard someone else say, even if it wasn't directed at you. Then, with all the strength you can muster, all the courage you can find, take a deep breath and know that you are safe. Find comfort in that thought, take another breath and think it again. Repeat this until you are at peace. And if this is all you can do or know to do at this moment, then by all means, do it.

By Renae Sauter, Clinical Therapist

A special thanks to Kellie Fitzgerald who wanted me to say a few words in this amazing collaborative book on Suicide, as well all the other writers whose stories moved me to tears.

As both and educator and a therapist, the topic of depression and suicide is one that I am very familiar with. As an educator it is my job to educate my students on the biology of the brain and specifically depression as a medical disorder. As a therapist it is my job to screen for clinical depression and suicidality every time I meet with a client and I have met with thousands over the ten year span I have worked in a trauma center.

In working with clients as well as students I am met with a lot of resistance to depression being a real medical disorder. Even though I provide the education, the disbelief and stigma still remains in some cases. In fact even in cases where people are reporting to me that they are actively suicidal they still resist the education and the referral to a doctor, opting to remain with thoughts of suicide vs. taking on the wide varieties of stigmas associated with mental illness. The stigma and the disbelief run very deep in our culture and this prevents people from viewing depression from a different perspective. Because this is the case we need a concentrated massive effort to try to prevent these devastating events from continuing to happen.

In 2010, depression was recognized worldwide by W.H.O. (World Health Organization) as the number one medical disorder, this over heart disease, cancer, diabetes. This is how prevalent clinical depression is. Depression, as was cited in one of the earlier stories, is almost always correlated with suicide. So if we can treat the depression we can prevent suicide from happening.

We all know when someone is in trouble. Don't hesitate to act on someone's behalf. Your local police will gladly perform a health and wellness check if you suspect someone you know is in danger. Just make the call.

Final thoughts from Kellie

I'd like to say, first off, thank you for reading this book and I hope it has in some small way helped you. These stories were purposely left "raw." Exactly as each author wrote them. This book is not intended to be a great literary work, rather to begin a discussion about mental illnesses, particularly depression, and suicide and the impact these things have on each and every one of us whether or not we've battled depression or lost someone to suicide ourselves.

Since we never really know exactly what someone else is going through "behind closed doors" I ask that each and every one of us strive to be more compassionate, more caring and more patient so that we really listen to what someone is really saying rather than simply hearing their voice. Sometimes something as simple as being an understanding sounding board without any judgment at all makes all the difference.

If you find someone you love is becoming withdrawn, or acting in a manner not consistent with who you know them to be, or who simply says they've considered suicide even if they claim to have been joking, please ask questions. Let them know you are there for them if they need to talk. Let them know it's OK for them to feel sad or angry or even depressed and that you will help them find the help they need to feel better. Tell them you love them and want them to be happy.

Since so many people who battle with depression have been known to take extreme measures to hide their private battle, it's really important to pay attention if you feel they might be having a really difficult time. Often someone who is depressed will hide their depression behind a jovial comic's mask. Or they might simply do silly things or try to make everyone around them laugh. If something doesn't feel "right" to you about someone else's sudden desire to be a comedian...pay attention. Again, ask questions, be a friend. You might just be saving someone's life. It really IS that serious.

www.ingramcontent.com/pod-product-compliance
Lightning Source LLC
Chambersburg PA
CBHW072056290426
44110CB00014B/1704